DATE DUE

MAI AUG 1 0 1989		
MAI AUG 2 4 1989		
MAI SEP 1 6 1989		
MAI NOV 0 4 1989		
MAI APR 0 1 1992		

Draw **50**
Monsters, Creeps,
Superheroes,
Demons, Dragons,
Nerds, Dirts, Ghouls,
Giants, Vampires,
Zombies, and
Other Curiosa...

LEE J. AMES

Draw **50**

Monsters, Creeps, Superheroes, Demons, Dragons, Nerds, Dirts, Ghouls, Giants, Vampires, Zombies, and Other Curiosa...

Doubleday & Company, Inc.
Garden City, New York

ISBN: 0-385-17637-6 Trade
ISBN: 0-385-17638-4 Prebound
ISBN: 0-385-17639-2 Paperback
Text copyright © 1983 by Lee J. Ames and Murray D. Zak

Library of Congress Cataloging in Publication Data

Ames, Lee J.
  Draw 50 monsters, creeps, superheroes, demons, dragons, nerds, dirts, ghouls, giants, vampires, zombies and other curiosa . . .

  Summary: Step-by-step instructions for drawing monsters and other assorted creatures. Includes Darth Vader, Frankenstein, the Hunchback of Notre Dame, and Jaws.
  1. Monsters in art — Juvenile literature. 2. Animals, Mythical, in art — Juvenile literature. 3. Drawing — Technique — Juvenile literature. [1. Monsters in art. 2. Drawing — Technique] I. Title. II. Title: Draw fifty monsters, creeps, superheroes, demons, dragons, nerds, dirts, ghouls, giants, vampires, zombies and other curiosa . . .
  NC825.M6A47   1983   741.2'4   80-3006
  9 8 7 6 5

To the jokesters down at Whaler's
and to Walter, loved so well...

Thanks, Holly!
Thanks, Tamara!
Thanks to Doug Bergstreser for the idea.

To the Reader

A wild and wacky collection of monsters and other fantastic creatures awaits you in this book, and by following simple, step-by-step instructions, you can draw each and every one of them, from the Bride of Frankenstein to Sasquatch.

Start by gathering your equipment. You will need paper, medium and soft pencils, and a kneaded eraser (available at art supply stores). You may also wish to have on hand India ink, a fine brush or pen, and a compass.

Next, pick the creature of your choice — you need not start with the first illustration. As you begin, keep in mind that the first few steps — the foundation of the drawing — are the most important. The whole picture will be spoiled if they are not right. So, follow these steps *very carefully,* keeping the lines as light as possible. So that they can be clearly seen, these lines are shown darker in this book than you should draw them. You can lighten your marks by gently pressing them with the kneaded eraser.

Make sure step one is accurate before you go on to step two. To check your own accuracy, hold the work up to a mirror after a few steps. By reversing the image, the mirror gives you a new view of the drawing. If you haven't done it quite right, you may notice that your drawing is out of proprotion or off to one side.

You can reinforce the drawing by going over the completed final step with India ink and a fine brush or pen. When the ink has dried, gently remove the pencil lines with the kneaded eraser.

Don't get discouraged if, at first, you find it difficult to duplicate the shapes pictured. Just keep at it, and in no time you'll be able to make the pencil go just where you wish. Drawing, like any other skill, requires patience, practice, and perseverance.

Remember, this book presents only one method of drawing. In a most enjoyable way, it will help you develop a certain skill and control. But there are many other ways of drawing to which you can apply this skill, and the more of them you explore, the more interesting your drawings will be.

Lee J. Ames

To the Parent or Teacher

The ability to make a credible, amusing, or attractive drawing never fails to fill a child with pride and a sense of accomplishment. This in itself provides the motivation for a child to cultivate that ability further.

There are diverse approaches to developing the art of drawing. Some contemporary ways stress freedom of expression, experimentation, and self-evaluation of competence and growth. More traditional is the "follow me, step-by-step" method which teaches through mimicry. Each approach has its own value, and one need not exclude the other.

This book teaches a way of drawing based on the traditional method. It will give young people the opportunity to produce skillful, funny drawings of monsters and other creatures by following simple instructions. After completing a number of such drawings, the child will almost surely have picked up some of the fundamentals of handling and controlling the materials and of creating believable forms, and a sense of the discipline needed to master the art of drawing. From here, the child can continue with other books in the DRAW 50 series — and at the same time, explore other methods of drawing which he or she will now be better equipped to deal with.

Werner Werewolf

UR2EZ

The Bride of Frankenstein

Romney Horrorfield, demon

Hippus maximus centaurus

Sasquatch

Super Itch

Bugg O'Neer

Rashid the Rotten

Wynsomme Warthead, witch

Yoda

Reeko Mortis, zombie

Medusa

Darth Vader

Marv Gryphon

Murt the Dirt

Gabba Ghoul

Lewis E. Furr

Wee Seamus Kildare, leprechaun

Jaws

Egeni Chillingstone, warlock

Ezobite mouth creach

Dracula

Sinister Finster, dark demon

Feodor the Dwarf

Quicksilver

Clipper Gyp

Demon from the Second Planet Circling Sirius

Frankenstein's Monster

Rory LaGoon

Cyclops

Fong Choy Noon

The Hunchback of Notre Dame

Lousy Larrabee

Bluddin Gaur, zombie

Burt the Dirt

Vilma Knibblenecker

Nose creach from Brinza

Ezobite eye creach

Dunston Dripp, nasal nerd

The Phantom of the Opera

John Henry

Bad Bjorn, giant troll

Uriah Creep

Sillawarsh, undiscovered slime monster

Crullbeef Oryu Creep

Kurt the Dirt

Super Cowboy

Lee J. Ames has been earning his living as an artist for almost forty years. He began his career working on Walt Disney's *Fantasia* and *Pinocchio.* He has taught at the School of Visual Arts in Manhattan and, more recently, at Dowling College on Long Island. He was, for a time, director of his own advertising agency and illustrator for several magazines. Mr. Ames has illustrated over one hundred books, from preschool picture books to postgraduate texts. When not working, he relaxes on the tennis court. A native New Yorker, Lee J. Ames lives in Dix Hills with his wife, Jocelyn, their three dogs, and a calico cat.